Make it YOUR Mark

7 Steps to Maximize Your Impact

Susan Gonzales

Leave a Purposeful and Lasting Impression

Susan Gonzales Enterprises L.L.C.
P.O. Box 701727
San Antonio, Texas 78270
888-999-3145
susan@makeityourmark.com
www.MakeItYourMark.com

Limits of Liability and Disclaimer of Warranty

The author and publisher shall not be liable for your misuse of this material. This book is strictly for informational and educational purposes.

Warning – Disclaimer

The purpose of this book is to educate and entertain. The author and/or publisher do not guarantee that anyone following these techniques, suggestions, tips, ideas, or strategies will become successful. The author and/or publisher shall have neither liability nor responsibility to anyone with respect to any loss or damage caused, or alleged to be caused, directly or indirectly by the information contained in this book.

Make it YOUR Mark

One Day at a Time...

Get your FREE Tools and Resources

www.MakeItYourMark.com

"You already hold the key to success, you just have to look within to unlock your fortunes."

Susan Gonzales

Here's a sampling of what you'll find:

- Personal Development Tools
- Inspirational Messages
- Podcasts, Articles and Resources
- Meet the Author Events
- Surprise Live Chats with Susan

PLUS:

Learn how you can attend a live "Make it YouMark™" training or bring one to your organization or local area!

www.MakeItYourMark.com

Acknowledgements

I would like to thank the many people who made this book possible.

First, to all my family and friends who encouraged me to go for it, and without whose support this book would still be just an idea and a topic of conversation for years to come.

To my husband, Steve, for cherishing and supporting me every day, especially over the past six months as I was writing. I love you dearly.

To my sons, Joey and Jimmy, for all their love and belief in me. I am blessed to have you both in my life. Thanks for the playlists to keep me focused, for the suggestions to make sure my voice showed up in the stories, and for the laughs.

To my daughter-in-law Nina for her support, assistance and promotion of my efforts.

To my dear friend Sylvia for her encouragement, wit, kindness, and love of life and her keen knowledge of comma placement!

To all my guardian angels, teachers, mentors and coaches who left a lasting imprint of inspiration and authenticity in my life.

To those who graciously provided their stories for inclusion in this book, especially John Bond, Sean Crosby and Jerry Trevino.

To my parents and all my siblings who still tell some of the best stories ever. You have all had a major influence in my life.

My heartfelt thanks to each of you!

About the Author

Susan Gonzales is a creative, fun loving trainer, professional coach, mentor, and distinguished speaker.

With over 20 years of senior level experience in business and talent development, she is highly regarded as an agent of change with a people first approach.

She is the CEO of Susan Gonzales Enterprises L.L.C. and creator of the Make it YOUR Mark™ personal growth and development system.

After surviving childhood trauma, divorce, diabetes, and practically losing herself in the process, Susan received what she calls "a life jolting wake-up call". She finally got it – that our time is not infinite and now is the time for LIVING. No matter what circumstances we experience in life, we have tremendous greatness within ourselves to take the lead in our life, make our mark, and happily live on our own terms.

Inspired by her realization, she transformed her approach and quickly became an inspirational force in her life and career as a leader, professional coach, and speaker. Since then, she has dedicated her life to helping others connect to their passion and greatness, to make their mark and share their voice with the world.

Contents

Prologue

The Creator gathered all of Creation and said,

*"I want to hide something from the humans until they are ready for it. It is the realization that **they create their own reality."***

The eagle said, "Give it to me, I will take it to the moon."

The Creator said, "No. One day they will go there and find it."

The salmon said, "I will bury it on the bottom of the ocean."

"No. They will go there too."

The buffalo said, "I will bury it on the Great Plains."

The Creator said, "They will cut into the skin of the Earth and find it even there."

Grandmother Mole, who lives in the breast of Mother Earth, and who has no physical eyes but sees with spiritual eyes, said,

"Put it inside of them."

*And the Creator said, **"It is done."***

Introduction

There are different approaches to measuring self-worth. Sometimes it's measured by accomplishments or wealth, other times it's measured by overcoming challenges and struggles, or in the impact had in someone's life.

But sooner or later, in one way or another, most will look back on life and wonder:

What is my legacy? What bit of evidence did I leave behind that says, I was here?

Some leave their unique mark in the form of a masterpiece on canvas or a sculpture on the side of a mountaintop. Others make a mark in the classroom impressing thousands of minds.

Still others make a mark in the shared stories that transport us to a place of new ideas, wonder and imagination, hope and connection to our dreams and wishes.

I come from a long line of story tellers. I grew up in a very large family of ten children and most times the drama around our kitchen table was so entertaining, we didn't need TV.

So it's no surprise that I tend to fall in the story teller group.

Like others, I have experienced the loss of loved ones in my family, unexpected career changes and financial ups and downs. I have failed at so many things the first go round and had to learn some lessons the very hard way.

Each time I was knocked down, I was lucky enough to connect to someone who had overcome adversity far worse than mine or someone who could be considered an inspirational muse.

These people shared stories that came from the heart and allowed me to see the mark of the person, the imprint of their purpose.

I consider them guardian angels and life teachers, because at these important junctures in my journey, they brought me great awareness and made a powerful impact in my life.

The lessons they taught are so vital, that I have compiled them into 7 steps that I call Critical Connections. You can even consider them as a way for you to "connect the dots" to create your blueprint or map to your purpose.

I pass on some of my favorite stories and the corresponding Critical Connections in the following chapters to those of you who are in "hard lesson" mode, or those of you looking for inspiration as you journey on to live your best possible life.

As you dive in, I invite you to consider the times you get asked about your story, especially in social settings. People are usually curious about who they are meeting and they ask questions that might sound like these:

"What's your story?"

"Tell me a little about yourself."

"What do you do?"

"How'd you come to be a part of this?"

And the questions go on and on. Usually when asked these questions, you tell the story that you feel is appropriate for the situation or what I refer to as the "social tale."

This social tale can also be the story that others have formed of you and can become so engrained in your thoughts that you take it on as your reality.

But as I have experienced so many times, deep down inside is the real story that is waiting to be told. Told in your authentic voice, one that connects the "missing" links of the social tale to your desired reality.

Your true story, the one you want the world to know about you, can also transport you. It can transport you to the place where you want to be - To WHO you want to be. From going through the motions; to living your purpose and making your mark.

Instead of "once upon a time" yours begins with two simple questions:

Who do you want to be?

And how do you want to show up?

Your purpose. Your mark.

1

Not a Chair Dancer Anymore

Dance like no one is watching. Love like you'll
never be hurt. Sing like no one is listening.
Live like it's heaven on earth.

Susanna Clark and Richard Leigh

I worked with this amazing person who was by far the nicest person I've ever met. He seemed to genuinely care about people and in turn, people just loved him. Usually when his name was mentioned, a smile would appear on the person's face and they would say things like:

"John Bond. Oh, he is so nice. I just love him."

"John has a great playlist and he will share it with you because he really is a good guy!"

"If I'm in a bad mood, I just go see John and I always feel so much better afterwards."

John was humble and did not talk about himself very much in terms of ego, but he did show how kind and caring he was in his actions with people every day.

Sometimes they were small random acts of kindness and sometimes they were major, life changing acts. Like donating a kidney to someone he didn't even know because he heard they might die and he was a match.

But with all this love and regard from others, John was a puzzle to me because there was a nervous side to him as well. He seemed to keep himself buttoned up tightly all the way to the top button on his shirt and the cuffs on his sleeves.

The way he presented himself at work and especially with the leadership team just didn't seem to match the beautiful, playful spirit that I felt when I was with him.

At first I thought he was being overly polite, maybe even a little subservient in his interactions. But as I began to interact more and more with him, I realized that the real John was bound up tightly and not allowed to come out and play while he was at work.

He held back on saying things that needed to be said or would be so nervous when he did speak up, that even though what he was saying was phenomenal, it was missed by the listeners.

John had been chosen to attend the coach training program that I led and the story began to change. During one of the training "dance" breaks, I noticed that John's facial expression indicated that he was into the song, but his body wasn't.

So right then I decided to get to know the authentic John Bond.

"This is a great song John", I said as I danced over to him.

"Yes it is! I love music!" he said with a huge grin on his face, yet his feet were barely moving on the floor and his hands were so close to his body it was as if they were invisibly tied down. People could have thought he needed dance lessons the way he was moving.

"C'mon John, I know you can dance and this kind of shuffling doesn't do you justice. I know there is a music man inside you".

"You have no idea, sister. I actually have a full dance studio at home, with a disco ball and laser lights. I can move!" he said playfully, giving me a little taste of his dancing moves.

"I knew it! I knew you had moves. Why in the world are you holding back here? Bring out the dancer and let's have some fun."

"No, no...I can't do that here. I think some of the supervisors wouldn't think it appropriate".

Then he abruptly walked to the other side of the room and I felt a little sad that John felt so repressed. All I could think about was the Broadway musical "Billy Elliot", because in the play being a dancer was not an acceptable male profession in his town and all Billy wanted to do was dance.

Months had gone by and even though John was laughing more, he still wasn't playing full out. Then, I fell down the stairs at work and injured my leg. I had a large training coming up and so I asked John if he could assist as I couldn't stand for long periods. Of course, being the nice person that he is, he said yes.

When it came to dance break time, I jokingly told the participants,

"I am with you in spirit, but will have to settle for 'dancing' from my chair."

Suddenly John pulled his chair next to mine and said,

"I don't dance, but I'll chair dance with you!"

I'd never seen him let loose like that, it was so different. His arms were swinging, his feet were tapping, and his whole body was moving to the beat of the music.

Of course, there was a safety net in dancing from the chair with a part of his body still restrained, yet the room just boomed with his energy. People who normally didn't join in the dance break, were up and laughing and strutting their stuff. A few others joined us in their chairs.

So our catch phrase became, "I'm a chair dancer!" I jokingly said this to him anytime I wanted the "real" John to come out and play. He would burst out laughing and loosen up by doing a little dance move to the side.

I eventually left that company to be the chief operating officer of an international coach training school, but stayed in contact with my friend. We talked often and he would tell me about feeling repressed and how he wanted to be his true self. I always responded,

"John, the world would be a better place if the real you came out to play. Just go for it!"

One day I was visiting and saw John at his office. It was one of the best days of my life because he came up to me so playfully and I noticed that his shirt was not buttoned up to his neck – oh my! He seemed so relaxed, in his own skin so to speak.

"Oh my god, John, you look so great and comfortable. I love it!"

Nudging me with his arm and grabbing me into a hug, he said,

"You want to know the best part?"

"Yes!"

"I'm not a chair dancer anymore! I am out of the chair and I dance now – really dance."

"What? This is fantastic! I am so happy for you and remember when you just sort of swayed from side to side?"

John then shared a part of the story that I hadn't known. He actually was a chair dancer in public, even when he used to go out with his friends. John would carry a chair out onto the dance floor to join the fun, but he just couldn't dance without a prop.

I found this information amazing. John shared,

"Even then I had to have a few drinks to do that. My friends didn't seem to care and they accepted me, but unless I was primed with a drink, I just couldn't dance in public."

What was so telling about this was John had such a desire to join in the fun, but was afraid to put down his guard and dance freely. Yet, he had the courage to carry a chair out onto the dance floor at clubs and join in the fun that way. When I mentioned the irony of this to him he replied,

"Well, I might have appreciated a little prodding to get me out of the chair when I was with my friends, but I don't think I was ready then."

"What do you think made it different or gave you the courage to just let go?"

"There was a level of fun and comfort when you were here. I felt that it was okay to let go and be myself when I was around you. A feeling and energy of freedom resonated around you and it was contagious."

John told me that it was like 'being given permission to be yourself' when he was with me. I created a feeling of safety and invitation to accept the fun side of himself and to play full out.

He said that he would see me and then ask himself,

"If she can do it, why can't I?"

One day, John cut the anchors that were holding him back. Without realizing it, he had moved away from the chairs and tables and danced in front of everyone in the middle of the room. From that point on there was no going back for him. He began living fully and dancing was just the tipping point.

"It was exhilarating and life changing for me and I keep a disco ball in my office as a constant reminder to be my true self, to live in the moment and to bring OUT the FUN."

I was so overwhelmed by what John shared with me and touched that he found me to be an inspiration, as I found his actions to be the inspiring ones.

Here was this courageous man, who did not hesitate to give his kidney to a stranger in need, who left a lasting imprint in my life and I guess the beauty of this is that I left one in his life too.

For his own personal reasons John had been playing small and kept his greatness buttoned up. But not anymore, he connected and linked his inner self with his outer persona.

Now he dances, freely and openly allowing others to get out of their chairs and embrace the true person within themselves - to liberate and share their greatness with the world.

2

Link the Inner to the Outer

You already hold the key to success.
You just have to look within to unlock
your fortunes.

Susan Gonzales

Critical Connection #1

Link the Inner to the Outer

1. Your Purpose, Your Mark
2. Vision, Values, Voice
3. The Purpose Zone
4. Your Ride So Far

Have you ever noticed that you can have lots of action plans and goals and still miss your mark?

Maybe you're like John Bond, in the previous chapter, who knew who he wanted to be, but was reluctant to let his outer manifestation mirror his true self for fear of judgment by others.

You might want to lose weight, even paid someone or joined a program, only to end up the same as you started or sometimes weighing even more.

It could be that you have a "To Do" list that is a mile long and even when you have the time, the big items never get crossed off.

You want to switch careers, but even though you might hate your current job you don't take any real action to make the change.

Why this seemingly never-ending lack of success or procrastination? There are inner forces, which have as much, if not more to do with your success than any of the outer manifestations.

There are emotional and spiritual components that impact thoughts and actions. These inner thoughts and emotions trigger different responses depending on our belief systems, the environment, our levels of stress, and so on.

When you *"link the inner to the outer"*, you have the ability to align your inner forces with your outer actions to make an impact, achieve success and live a full and satisfying life.

You become more aware of what you're thinking, feeling, and doing and so you increase your ability to make choices that are aligned with what you truly want and value, and the success you want to achieve.

Sometimes people equate success as achievements or accomplishments, seeking satisfaction or fulfillment from an outer perspective.

"If I get that promotion or make that rank, I will be more satisfied and more fulfilled."

"When I have my dream home, car, furniture...I will be happy."

But even though you keep achieving more and more, there could still be something missing. Outwardly you seem successful, but internally the level of fulfillment is never quite reached. It becomes clear that success without inner fulfillment can end up being the ultimate failure.

What gives you fulfillment? Only you can decide that and in actuality you are your own expert in this area.

But, what usually happens, is people want a formula so they can take action and get it done, like a checklist. They seek the outer reward.

Your Purpose – Your Mark

If you're focused on the outcome and it's not linked to your true purpose, a high level of fulfillment will be lacking, no matter how hard you try or work towards it.

When you look at the two questions posed in this book they encompass both inner and outer aspects:

Inner: Who do you want to be?

Outer: How do you want to show up?

They seem like simple questions, but in reality they are very complex. Who do you want to be? This is related to the spiritual and emotional components of your life – **your purpose**. How do you want to show up? This is related to the external aspects of what you do and say – **your mark.**

When you look at times in your life when you were in the "purpose zone", it was most likely because you had both of these areas in alignment – your actions matched your intent.

You've probably experienced purposeful moments or periods in your life but they do not last. Where did the alignment of your intent and actions go? What is stopping you from being in the "purpose zone" consistently?

Take a look at the inner component and focus on who you want to be. If you are not clear about your purpose, then it stands to reason that you'll have a difficult time sustaining action or achieving the highest levels of fulfillment.

For example, if you do not know who you want to be, then you could get off track by doing something that does not give you fulfillment.

You can rationalize with yourself about making it work, but your purpose isn't fully manifested – and deep down inside you know it – so you end up with rather lackluster performance or results and with feelings of resentment or apathy.

Which is why the critical connection between the inner and the outer is key to sustaining your success, making the changes you want, reaching your goals, and bringing your vision to reality.

3 Essential Elements

I've come to find, over the course of my experiences, as a corporate executive, leadership mentor, and professional coach, that there are three essential elements for living your purpose. I identify these elements as your vision, values and voice. Each element is briefly introduced in this chapter and then explored in a much deeper level in the following chapters.

Vision is the component that connects you both spiritually and emotionally to your untapped potential, so you realize the true wants and desires you have for your life. It helps you know where you want to go and what it will look like when you get there. When you align your vision to your truest wants and dreams, it pulls you forward to who you want to be and how you want to show up.

In John's case, he had a vision of who he was and what he wanted out of life, but he wasn't able to bring that vision to life which is why he continued to dance from the chair.

Values are the principles and beliefs you live by and represent your judgment of what is important in life. The things that make you tick, that drive you – like your own internal GPS. Values are at our core and they have the most impact on how you react emotionally because they are what you hold dear.

John had values that he held dear as well, which is why he gave his kidney to a stranger and why he was always willing to help others.

Voice is how you tell your true story, how you show up authentically. The way you represent your talents and gifts, those things that make you unique. A tremendous amount of influence is related to voice as it shows up as an outer action, but is deeply rooted to your values and vision. It's how you relate your purpose to yourself and others.

When everyone else was dancing and having fun, John was holding back in direct conflict with his value of contributing. He was so fun-loving and lighthearted and by playing small he was detracting from the total experience. Interesting that in some areas of his life, he was able to show up and speak openly and in this one area where he was vulnerable to rejection, he held back.

As John sat in the chair, part of his voice was missing and even though he had some fun, he knew that he wasn't really being true to himself.

The Purpose Zone

The picture above illustrates what I refer to as the purpose zone. It's like an inline skate with three wheels. When you are in the purpose zone, things roll along very nicely in integrity to your authentic self, because all three elements are intact.

But if one of these three wheels is missing or goes flat, your purpose ride starts to get wobbly and your purpose comes crashing down. When the link between the inner and the outer is broken, your actions become misaligned with your intentions, and you're prevented from showing up authentically and powerfully, which is what happened to John.

The good thing is, there has never been a better time for you to do a little maintenance, to make sure that you have all three wheels on your ride and that they are full of air and rolling smoothly. Then you can stay in the purpose zone and make your mark, leaving a lasting imprint on the people and places in your world.

Your Ride So Far

To get started, take a look at your ride so far, a review of your life to this point. What is working and what is not or areas where things were working fine previously, but now you're not as pleased or fulfilled anymore.

Give yourself time to take a look at the sweet spots as well as the tart or downright sour times. Right about now you might be feeling some unease about regrets you have or times in your life that you're not so proud of, times that you consciously chose something you knew wasn't good for you.

Don't worry, thoughts like that are pretty normal, and it's all part of the learning process.

If you're not sure how to get started, try using some of these questions and respond to the statements. Once you get going, add your own questions and answers.

1. *Describe yourself today – WHO you are now? How have you been showing up?*
2. *What fears do you have?*
3. *What regrets?*
4. *What gets in your way?*
5. *What lessons do you feel you still aren't quite learning or keep learning the hard way?*
6. *What do you daydream about?*
7. *List all the things you love about yourself.*
8. *In what areas of your life are you just settling or feel like you failed?*
9. *What is one unfilled dream you have?*
10. *What are you celebrating?*
11. *When do you feel like you can be your true self? When do you feel like you need to mask your true self?*

12. *What do you do?*
13. *What challenges or obstacles are you experiencing?*
14. *What is one thing that you would like to do over?*
15. *When was the last time you did something for the first time?*

As you progress through this book and learn more about the other Critical Connections, you can refer back to your review and make notes, additions, and other insights that come up for you.

When you become more aware, of the things that are working as well as the areas in your life that you want to have more success or fulfillment, you can make the choices that will close the gap between where you are now to where you want to be.

3

Now What?

Oh fudge! Only I didn't say fudge. I said THE word. The big one. The queen mother of dirty words. The F-dash-dash-dash word.

Ralphie, A Christmas Story 1983

You know the situation.

Successful career, feeling like you are at the top of your game, paid your dues and now you are finally reaping the rewards. Then suddenly the bottom falls out and you unexpectedly lose your job.

Well, yep something like that happened to me too.

What's it like to feel the rug pulled out from underneath you – when you are on a magic carpet high in the air? For me it was quite surreal.

For a few days I was on an emotional roller coaster: up with optimism and down with grief, up with possibilities and then down with anger, quickly followed by a surging ascent of "you can't keep me down" and then another major descent into fear and nausea.

Finally I landed in a still place of quiet reflection and then acceptance.

So there I was on the other side of fifty, and what I thought was my dream career was unexpectedly and abruptly at an end.

F-dash-dash-dash word! Now what? I asked myself.

As I sat there in the stillness, pondering my future, I realized something. It hit me – POW! Just like the "I could have had a V-8" commercial.

When the CEO unexpectedly told me that he was putting someone else in my position and wanted me to run a new division, I said without even pausing,

"I don't want that. My heart isn't in it."

I don't know who was more surprised by what I had just said, him or me. But in that moment, when I turned down the offer and in the next few days decided to leave the company, I had taken a courageous step in creating the reality that I wanted – one that was heartfelt and meaningful.

I had been playing it safe and small in that executive role and in so doing, had deferred my ideal vision to the proverbial "someday". I was making good money, but I was not fulfilled and I was subconsciously letting the security of my salary outweigh taking the big step into my true purpose.

I had slipped so deep into my comfort zone and had become so disconnected to what I really wanted in life, I was basically going through the motions. It was as if I was playing a supporting role in my own life story and even worse, I was using a script written by someone else with my true voice almost non-existent.

Deep in my heart I knew that my story was patiently waiting to be told in my authentic voice. I had been daydreaming and longing for it for years, and now it was time to take the lead role in my life.

The story that would transport me to the place where I wanted to be – to WHO I wanted to be.

I took the leap of faith and committed to creating my vision of a company that would be devoted to helping others live full and satisfying lives, which became Susan Gonzales Enterprises L.L.C.

I can now walk my talk and fully embrace the talents and gifts bestowed on me to engage with others who seek a more purposeful connection for their lives, helping them create their reality.

A reality that is aligned with their values, vision, and voice and one that will leave a lasting heartfelt impression on the people and places in their lives.

4

Be Still

*The self must know stillness before it can
discover its true song.*

Ralph Brum

Critical Connection #2

Be Still

1. Shh, Your Purpose is Calling
2. Getting Still
3. In the Moment Centering

Sometimes our lives are so hectic that we just step into get it done mode and completely disconnect from our vision and our values. This diminishes the power of our voice and it can even have the opposite effect of what we want.

It can be very difficult to hear your inner voice, if you are wrapped up in the "hecticness" of doing and not thinking, feeling or connecting to your vision.

Being still is about taking the time to calm your mind and refuel yourself so that you stay aligned with your values and gifts.

Shhh, Your Purpose is Calling

Stillness can be very difficult. When we stop and let go, our minds can have some pretty funky thoughts and the natural tendency is to shut them down. But, when your brain is full of noise, you can unconsciously block out your inner voice.

Those signs that so many are looking for to help guide them to their purpose can be missed in the chaotic clutter of our need to be incessantly moving.

This movement is just a diversionary tactic because the stillness is so uneasy and awkward, that you seek busy work to avoid the discomfort of your thoughts.

But since busy work isn't connected to your purpose, you're just marking time and not making a difference in your life. If you want to hear your purpose calling you, then having a quiet, still space in your brain can help you receive it loud and clear.

Once I allowed myself to be in a quiet, reflective place I made the connection to why my heart was no longer in it with the company I left as described in the previous chapter. I loved working there and I loved the people, and they loved me too. So on the people front it was great.

But on the creative, idea generating side it was lacking for me and I was feeling stale. I wanted to do so much more with my ideas and talents, so the buy-in wasn't there for me to want to lead another division. My heart wasn't in it – I had more to contribute than that and I was not willing to waste any more time.

Getting Still

How can you create a still quiet space in your brain especially with all the ways to stay plugged in nowadays?

There are lots of ways that you can find your stillness and you will want to choose the one that makes the most sense for you. Whatever your method, you want to make sure that you are intentionally being still for the purposes of clearing your mind to connect to your vision, values, and your voice.

You want to be able to hear any deep insights or messages that your inner self is sending you. By hear, I mean feel them and process them so you're fully aware of the decisions you make in regards to what the messages are telling you.

Some people, find their stillness when running and describe it as being in the zone. They connect to their breathing, and the steady fall of their feet hitting the ground creates an almost meditative state for them.

Others find it in their natural surroundings while sitting in their gardens or going to a favorite place in the park with a view of a meadow or river. Others find it by meditating daily for 30 – 45 minutes or more. They use recorded guided meditations or have their own chants and processes.

Still others find it when they pray or quietly reflect in their place of worship. Letting the silence of the space and the closeness to God relax and quiet their minds.

It is amazing how refreshed you can feel by just allowing your mind to pause for even a brief period of time.

In the Moment Centering

There are also ways to help you clear you mind in the moment. These might be related to a specific event or action or just for the purpose of bringing focus to something. Either way, they are powerful because, they will help you stay aligned to who you want to be and how you want to show up, at any given time.

So if full blown meditation isn't for you or you don't have 30 – 40 minutes during the day to devote to running or reflecting, a simpler approach could be just what you need.

The one that I have found to be the most effective is what I call "in the moment centering", which is a simple way to ground yourself and shift from hectic to calm in just a few minutes.

You can do this anytime, anywhere, as often as you like and if you're considering some kind of meditation in the future, this can be a small step towards a longer form of being still.

It can be as simple as having a mantra to instantly calm the brain, to be still in the moment, so you can show up the way you truly choose and want to be.

When you have a mantra, you use it to create a feeling that you want to have. If you want to be calm, choose a mantra that helps you feel calm. As you begin to use this technique you will want to take a few deep breaths and let them out slowly feeling your body begin to relax. Then say the mantra several times so that your brain connects the saying to the feeling you are trying to achieve. As you continue to use it, you will only have to think the mantra and the feeling should follow.

Here are some of the mantras that my clients have shared that you might find useful too:

- *Just stop.*
- *Quietly listening.*
- *De-stress and impress.*
- *Clear your mind and feel the quiet.*
- *This is for me.*
- *Be still.*
- *I'm ready.*
- *On the beach!*
- *Focus and finish.*

Once you have picked your mantra you will want to practice using it with the deep breathing often so that it will eventually just happen automatically.

Shhh...your inner voice is calling you.

5

I'm Here Now Dad

This is a story shared with me by Jerry Trevino Jr., a highly-regarded golf pro in Texas, who graciously offered to tell me about two major turning points in his life as we sat talking one day.

It started as a simple conversation, and then as most good conversations do, moved into some deep life lessons and experiences that actually took me by surprise in a very powerful way.

Here's the story in Jerry's words:

> I hope my son has opportunities to learn and grow from experiences like I did. I want him to make his own choices and have people in his life that encourage him to be his own man.

At this point in the conversation, we started to talk about Jerry's father, who had passed away unexpectedly, from a brain aneurysm. He had gone to play baseball with his kids in the evening and the next day was gone, leaving a loss still greatly felt by his family and friends.

> My dad had wanted to be a baseball star when he was young, but it didn't work out and I felt like he had pinned his hopes and dreams on me. I had always played several sports while I was growing up and once in a while my dad would take me to the golf course, but it was really just for fun.

> When I was in high school one of my dad's good friends kept encouraging me to take up golf in a more serious way. My dad would always say no - that baseball was my sport and I felt that way too. But in the back of my mind I was thinking that I would like to try golf with the same kind of focus I was putting into other sports.

> During this same time frame, my coach called all the athletes into the gym and said this was the last chance we had to change our sport. "So if you think you want to be on a different team or that this isn't for you – now is the time to speak up."

It was in that moment that I stood up and told the coach that I wanted to switch to golf. He looked a little surprised, but agreed that I should do what was in my heart. So that was good, but I wasn't sure how my dad was going to feel about it.

That night I told him and he was fine with it and pretty much said the same thing as my coach – to go with what was in my heart. He even started to put some serious effort into his own golf game to show his support of me. In that moment, he taught me that it was okay to make my own choices and decisions and he did it with his actions, not just his words. That's a pretty big lesson for a 16 year old to learn.

As Jerry shared a few more anecdotes about his dad, he started to tear up and as men usually do, tried to brush it off, but the emotion kept showing up. Then he told me the greatest lesson he learned and the one thing he wanted his dad to know – the one thing he wished he could tell him in person.

I loved golf, but for many years had hated my schedule as a golf pro – you know it was 7 days a week, 12 – 14 hour days and really no downtime and I missed so much. I felt the inner conflict of juggling my professional life and my personal.

My siblings wanted me to attend birthday parties and family functions because we're a tight knit family and even though my wife never pressured me, I knew she would have loved to spend more time with me.

I truly wanted to do it all, but I was tired. Then there was my dad, who just wanted me to spend some time playing golf with him."

My dad really liked to talk, and he would call me often, but I just didn't have time for long conversations and I would usually cut him off. I can't count the number of times he called to see if I could meet him for a round of golf and I said no because I was too busy.

Then my dad died just like that. Funny thing is, I did make time to play a round of golf with him two days before he passed, and I am glad for that. But, all those other times when he asked were gone forever and there wasn't going to be another day.

"That's when I knew I had to make a change", he said with a break in his voice.

I want my dad to know that I got the lesson he was trying to teach – that I am here now Dad. My job would no longer come before everything else. Even though I missed it while he was alive, now I got it.

I didn't want to waste any more time, because it can be gone in an instant, and I started to look at options for a new career. Then, I unexpectedly fell into an opportunity. One that would allow me to continue to be a golf pro and have more control over my schedule.

There was just one small catch, I had to attend a 10 day training session and it was going to be intense with a lot of reading and writing involved.

This's when I mastered the second lesson that my dad had taught me and to this day is one of the most important turning points for me.

I can't really read or write and have struggled with dyslexia my whole life. Most people don't know that about me because I have developed such great coping skills.

When I get a new client, they fill out the information card completely and if I need to write something, I usually just ask them to spell it out for me. Most people do it without even pausing or realizing that I don't write anything down. The new voice apps have been a God send to me because of the voice to text option, otherwise I would take forever to decipher the texts people send me.

Well I had to make a decision now, to pass up this amazing offer or to take a stand and be true to myself. When I shared my concerns about being able to complete the training with the owner, he acted like it was no big deal and said he would let the trainers know so I wouldn't be embarrassed.

I felt pretty good then and wasn't too concerned about handling the training, just the normal excitement of meeting the other team members and hoping we would all be a good fit.

The first morning of the training, the facilitator takes out the manual, and tells us that we're going to take turns reading portions of it aloud, then we'll discuss it.

Oh shit, I thought. This is my worst nightmare coming true. Now I'm sweating bullets and trying to pay attention to what's being read aloud, since that is the only way I am going to be able to learn it, while at the same time trying to figure out what section I'll have to read.

The trainer is randomly picking people and I'm thinking this isn't going very well. I really need to focus on the part that's being read, but my attention is so split that I can't. Then it happens, he calls my name.

"Jerry, why don't you go next and read this section."

I'm thinking – now what do I do? I looked up at the instructor and then down at the page, up again and then down – my mind racing. I can try and read this and stumble all over it and no one will learn anything or stop coping and just own it.

Right now in this moment, stop running from the dyslexia and take the opportunity presented to me to be my true self – vulnerabilities and all – to go with what was in my heart.

So I said, *"I can't."*

The trainer said, *"Oh, why not? Did you forget your glasses?"*

"Uh No, I can't read. I have a bad case of dyslexia."

Without missing a beat the trainer said, *"Well okay – would it help if I read it for you then?"*

"Yes!" I said in a very relieved tone.

The rest of the training the other participants offered to read aloud for me and to help make sure I didn't miss out on anything. No one made a big deal out of it – no one acted like they felt sorry for me – they just took it in that reading wasn't going to be my strong suit. I knew I was in the right place.

What started out as my worst nightmare coming true, ended up being a milestone for me, a point in my life where I was fully present and accepting of myself. The point in time, where I stood up and took a chance on being real and followed what was in my heart. The culmination of the lessons my dad was still teaching me.

That first year I surpassed all the sales goals and measures for the company and set records that still stand today. I also surpassed my own goals of making time for my family, fully connecting in the moment and being there.

Speaking with deep conviction and passion, Jerry shared,

I won't ever go back to the way I was before. I regret not spending time with my dad, but I will keep the lesson of "missed opportunities" and "being true to yourself" close to my heart. Now when my dad is looking down he can see that I show up, that I got it and that I am sharing it with my son.

I wish I could tell him in person, but I think he knows I got it, that - I am here **now,** Dad.

6

Choose Your Values

---

*They know what matters, but
they don't choose it...*

*The hardest thing on earth is to
choose what matters.*

Sue Monk Kidd, Secret Life of Bees

Critical Connection #3

Choose Your Values

1. Inherited vs. Chosen
2. When Values Clash
3. The Purpose Zone
4. Defining and Prioritizing

Values are the second component needed in fulfilling your purpose and being in the zone consistently. Values are the guiding principles you live by, the things that drive you and make you tick. Your judgment of what is important in life.

They are like an internal compass or GPS for your life, guiding your choices.

Values include things like integrity, honesty, charity, spirituality, physicality, respect, family, being loving, loyalty, open-minded, accepting, faithful, courteous, fairness, ingenuity, frugality....

Think of all the decisions and life choices you make. Decisions like the one Jerry faced in determining his priorities in the last chapter-to spend time with his Dad or work, to speak up and reveal his inability to read or to hide it.

If you're unaware of, or become disconnected with your values, you could end up making decisions and choices that no longer guide you in the direction you really want to take.

Inherited vs Chosen Values

Did you ever wonder where you really got your values? You probably inherited a great many of them from your parents or care givers as you were growing up. But you just as likely adopted some unconsciously as you began to experience life on your own. For the most part you were probably good with the majority of these values and they served you well.

As you've grown and experienced life and new environments, you might find that some values that you inherited or adopted, no longer align with who you've become.

Perhaps it's the definition that needs to be tweaked, the value needs to be re-prioritized or you may find that now you have a different belief altogether.

To get started, do a review of your own values. Think about the values you hold most dear and make a written list. Then take a look at the times when values seem to cause conflict or clash against each other.

When Values Clash

Usually when your actions and behaviors align with your values, life rolls along smoothly and contently. But when things aren't lining up with your values, that's when it can feel and go wrong.

Sometimes you find people who say they have the same value as you but in action it doesn't quite translate the same way.

For example, if you value respect and someone says something that makes you think they don't respect you, you'll have an emotional reaction – get upset or angry.

The interesting point that is usually missed in this situation, is understanding the intent of the other person. Was their intent to disrespect or were they working under a different definition of respect altogether? You may know your definition of your values, but don't assume that it is the same as everyone else's.

It's how conflict starts and breeds in many situations. Someone's value is not being honored, they take offense, and then it spirals down. Sometimes it's easy to remedy and sometimes it results in contention and disagreement that stagnates.

I see it all the time in organizations and companies when they try to nail down their core values. It can look something like this:

At XYZ we value integrity, honesty, responsibility, work ethic, and service.

Everyone agrees and the leaders pat themselves on the back for the good job they did. Then some time goes by and the employees are saying things like:

"Integrity my ass."

"Honesty – you got to be kidding me!"

"What's the point of having values if they don't walk the talk?"

What happened? Everyone saw the values and agreed that these were the most important, right?

It depends on how each person interpreted the meaning of the value. Honesty is good one to use for an example. Say you have two people who agree that honesty is their #1 value.

Person 1: Honesty means gut wrenching, brutal truth no matter what the circumstances.

Person 2: Honesty means being truthful as long as it doesn't hurt someone's feelings.

It is easy to see how their definitions of honesty do not align and this is how *Person 1* could assume that *Person 2* doesn't walk the talk. It's not really a value clash, but a lack of understanding of the meaning of the value to each person.

Another common value clash that many of my clients struggle with is work/life balance. Jerry's story from the last chapter, highlights this scenario. He thought his number one value was family, yet he found himself pulled away from home often and worked very long hours, even on the weekends. No time to talk on the phone with his dad and no time for a quick round of golf either.

Jerry's definition of family was providing a stable home for his wife, being a solid breadwinner, making sure there was money to support his future plans for becoming a father - college, braces, camp, etc.

No wonder there was a bit of a clash between his actions and the amount of time he was spending with his family.

It wasn't until his father unexpectedly passed away, that Jerry reflected on how he missed his mark in this case. He had unconsciously put his job as the number one priority to achieve his outcome.

He had the jolting realization that the material things were important, but actually being there – in person – experiencing his family and making an imprint in their lives was his top priority in valuing his family.

Once he aligned his value with his actions he was able to transform his life and create the balance that he truly desired.

Defining and Prioritizing Your Values

So many of life's decisions are about determining what you value the most. Getting clear on the definition and precedence you give your values, will help guide your choices in any situation. Choose from your heart, and from the vision you have created.

Be real and honest with this one. Your definition of what these mean and how you will act if you are living your values will leave a lasting mark on you and in the lives of others. Consider the impact you want to have and the imprint you want to leave.

Then, once you have compiled your list you need to write out what each of these values represents to you, how you define it. It helps to write out a description of the value in action to help you fully flush out the details.

Here's an example to get you started and then you can develop it as you go. Say you choose "responsibility" as one of your values:

I define responsibility as being accountable, trustworthy, committed and reliable.

I demonstrate the value of being responsible in my actions when I own up to my mistakes, make and keep my appointments and deadlines, put my all into completing tasks, and when I speak up if we are off track or when I need help.

Again, try to get as detailed as possible, because as you write out the definitions you'll find that some of the values you listed can actually be combined into one.

For instance if you value charity, generosity, and service you might combine them into one – philanthropy

Once you have defined and combined your values into a list of about ten, you will need to do the final prioritization and decide out of the ten which will be your top 3-5 core values.

Visit your values often and make adjustments as you need to, so your actions stay aligned with who you want to be and how you want to show up. Keep in mind that your values might change as you grow and mature.

Values impact every facet of your life including how you interact with people, your decisions and the choices you make that eventually determine the quality of your life. By consciously choosing and defining them you will keep the values' wheel inflated, supporting your vision, voice and upholding your purpose.

7

Don't Let the Hill Beat You

"Sue, I have cancer." I will never forget those words. My brother David had just been diagnosed with stage 4 cancer, and the doctors said he didn't have long to live. He was my big brother, and I still cannot write about him without crying. Cancer sucks!

In typical sister fashion I wanted to take action to cure him, but that wasn't possible. The best I could do was to make him feel better by perhaps taking his mind off the day to day drudgery of medical treatments – *that fucking cancer.*

Believing in the power of positive energy, I wanted to connect, to battle or endure with him, because just watching him wasn't enough- I needed to match the herculean effort he was putting into his battle.

So, what could I do that would be herculean? It had to be something that he would not expect me to do, something that was really hard for me, which had a physical component to it. I chose running in a marathon because for me running had always been torturous – beneficial, but so challenging for me.

That next day I started my quest to train and all I could do was shuffle run. *You know, when you're so tired that you can barely lift your feet, but you don't want to stop, so you fake like you're running, but really you're just shuffling along.* But I didn't care, if I had to crawl that's what I would do.

Every day, I went to the track and did my shuffle run for as long as I could. Soon my shuffle runs went from 5 minutes to 10 minutes, to 15 minutes, to actually jogging. Once I built up some stamina, I started running (I use this term very loosely) in the park to simulate what the actual event would feel like.

Oh the escapades I had and the great athletic moves I developed! Let's see, there was the "bent over double" which is a deep breathing move for when you feel like you might pass out or worse lose your lunch.

My all-time favorite was "the windmill" which happens when you're running along and trip on a root, then your feet go up in the air, and your arms start flailing in circles to prevent the inevitable tumble into the dirt.

David used to laugh so much when I shared all my stories of tripping and falling when I was running – damn roots! And, he was so proud when I told him that I beat my time by doing a 14 minute mile. Woo-Hoo, there's one for the record books!

On the day of the race, it was over 100 degrees in Texas, and I was in the last leg. I put my all into it, but I had never run in a race or on a course that was completely in the sun, so I was going pretty slowly. I was struggling with my pacing and breathing and I was already dreading the last leg of the run which was a really steep hill.

I kept pushing on, getting passed by most, and I started to rapidly fade. Some people were walking up the hill so I had to keep swerving around them and that wasn't helping my attitude either.

At this point, sweat was pouring into my eyes making it hard to see, and I was falling out of "the zone." I was starting to feel like I could not go on and was thinking:

"When is the excitement and energy of this race going to kick in? I am dying. Where is my second wind that everyone said I would get? Why is this so hard, I trained so much?"

Rubbing my Lance Armstrong "Live Strong" wrist band wasn't working to motivate me. Even scarier, thinking of David's struggle and how graciously he was "staying strong" wasn't working either. I became overwhelmed with guilt, because I was thinking of quitting.

Then, I heard a voice from the top of the hill holler out to me,

"#2746...DON'T LET THE HILL BEAT YOU!"

I looked up to see who was calling out, but I couldn't really make her out with the sweat stinging my eyes and with all the people in front of me.

It didn't even matter who said it because those words hit me like a lightning bolt right in my core. Fighting words –– **don't let** the hill beat you. I dug in and kept moving, but my pace really started to slow, and it took every ounce of willpower I had not to just walk the rest of the way. I was sure that I wouldn't make it up the hill.

Again, from the top of the hill, now several voices,

"#2746...YOU CAN DO THIS!"

"WALKERS, MOVE OVER. SOMEONE IS TRYING TO RUN UP THE HILL. MOVE OVER! MOVE OVER!"

The path in front of me started to clear, and again, but now a chorus of voices, I heard,

"#2746, DON"T LET THE HILL BEAT YOU! Dig deep, you can do this."

Now, I could see a large group of people in pink shirts (cancer survivors) cheering me on. I felt my brother so strongly at that moment. Somehow I found a burst of energy and suddenly I was at the top of the hill.

Cameras were in my face, and people were telling me to smile. I was so tired, and I was sure those pictures were going to be awful.

I thought I was at the finish line and the race was over, but I couldn't see the line to cross it.

"Where's the finish?" I gasped.

My guardian angels (that is how I think of them) pointed me in the right direction and said,

"You can do it. The finish line is still a ways off, but it is level, and you can do it."

I thought to myself (since I certainly couldn't talk at this point):

"What?! There's more?!...Holy Shit!"

In a stupor, I followed the waving arms pointing me in the right direction.

Finally, after what seemed like an eternity, I had the amazing feeling of crossing the finish line.

Pink shirts, fighters, winners, survivors, inspirers, people who I did not even know but would be forever grateful to for what they did that day.

They helped me give my brother David a break away from his cancer. When he saw the pictures that were taken as I made it to the top of the hill that day, he actually convulsed over into gut wrenching laughter that brought tears to his eyes.

Yes, as I predicted, I looked atrocious and so confused that even I fall over with laughter when I look at those pictures to this day.

My guardian angels gave me something that day too. They helped me realize that even when I think I can't, there's more. That even though I might have felt like I was racing all alone, there were people willing to help.

The help did not need to be a major ordeal, an inconvenience, or an imposition because all it took was just a cheering energy, a smiling face, and a point in the right direction to get me to the finish line.

To this day, it has become my mantra when I am faced with a difficulty or a challenge, or feel like I might quit on one of my dreams **– Don't let the hill beat you!**

We all have hills in our lives. Sometimes they can be little, sometimes they can seem like mountains. You too might be dreaming of conquering one of your own hills and feeling like you might want to stop. I invite you to use the mantra my guardian angels gave to me so you can persevere and reach your finish lines.

You might be thinking that the hill beat my brother, but you would be wrong.

He never stopped embracing the fun in life as he journeyed forward. On his terms, his way – with love and humor to the end. Leaving his lasting imprint in my heart and in the hearts of so many others.

8

Dream Big and Dig In

Trust Yourself.
Create the kind of self that you will be happy to
live with all of your life.

Make the most of yourself by fanning the tiny,
inner sparks of possibility into flames of
achievement.

Golda Meir

Critical Connection #4

Dream Big and Dig In

1. Dream Big Benefits
2. Vision Without Limits
3. Dig In!

Whether it is for an overall vision of your idyllic life or for a specific goal, like the one I had for supporting my brother, the first step is to dream big and the second is to dig in until you get it.

Dream Big

Why dream big? It helps you create a vision of where you want to go and what it will look like when you get there.

Another benefit from dreaming big is that it opens you up to possibilities, which equals opportunities. All of a sudden it can feel like something just fell in your lap. Or perhaps you achieve something despite overwhelming odds to the contrary.

You might be thinking, "What luck!" But, there could be more going on here than you realize. Ever heard of the saying, "Energy attracts like energy"?

Well that law of attraction from the study of quantum physics has a lot to do with the "all of a sudden all these great things are happening. Energy puts out a frequency and the energy associated with being open is very positive. When you are in opportunity mode or in the words of the quantum physicists – when your energetic frequency is attuned to opportunity – that is what you attract. So, things just seem to fall in your lap!

Also, big dreams push your comfort boundaries out to a wider learning space, providing even more power to your vision and the reality you want to create.

This vision can pull you forward to who you want to be and how you want to show up. For example, when you find yourself daydreaming of a better life, you are subconsciously tapping into your unlimited potential and greatness. This unlimited potential and greatness is who you really are at the core of your being but for some reason, you are limiting it in your current situation.

Vision, Without Limits

Just like being still can be uncomfortable, visioning can also bring out some jittery feelings which might tend to make you dismiss your vision as being too far out – too outrageous - too imaginary.

The tendency is to push down the potential with limiting thoughts like:

"This won't get you anywhere. You've got to keep your feet on the ground".

"Fantasy is fine, but it won't feed my kids."

"Sounds good, but how the heck do I make it come true?"

"There's no way I can ever have that."

The act of dreaming big and visioning your ideal life, is the first step in getting what you want out of life and making the contribution you desire.

You don't want to put any limits on this as you are creating because you might leave some great ideas out. Fantastic inventions, cures for diseases, and humanitarian efforts all started with an outrageously big dream.

What would you do if you won the lottery? This question sparks some of the best "daydreaming" responses and can be a way to free up your mind to be open to the potential that you want to tap into.

This question makes it safe because it can seem like a game, but the responses are actually tied to your true desires and wishes.

Ever woken up from a beautiful dream, disappointed when you woke, because the dream evoked such vivid imagery and feelings that it seemed real?

That's the same concept to keep in mind as you create your vision of your ideal life. See and feel a new future and paint the picture in your mind as if it's already happened. The more heart you put into it, the more success you'll have in bringing it to life.

Go BIG! This isn't the time to play small. Expand your boundaries, think the impossible, the ideal, and most excellent life in the world. This is the time to play and imagine, fantasize your dream of paradise. What is the dream that you have been ignoring or too afraid to attempt?

Once you have a fully drawn out vision of what you want, then you can start the process of planning the action steps to get you there.

Remember when you are in the purpose zone, your actions match your intent, which is why you want to get very clear on what you want in your vision. Once your vision is in motion, it can then leave the mark you intended.

There's something else about visioning, it changes with time and as you grow, it might have morphed into something very different from when you started. Visit your dream often so it stays aligned with your wants and desires and so it continues to pull you forward.

Dig In

Now, as you begin to move from visioning to putting things in action, it's not uncommon to doubt yourself or to feel like giving up.

Beware the naysayers! Too often those who are closest to you can inadvertently implant limiting beliefs into your thinking. Your big dream might be scary to them, which is fine – just don't take on their fears as your own.

These limiting beliefs can slowly erode your confidence and instill fear and doubt, which are major obstacles to achievement.

Keep in mind that big visions dump you right out of your comfort zone. With everything feeling so foreign to you, you could be tempted to slide back into what you know.

Maybe you feel the hill's too steep and you feel like you don't have anything left in your tank.

That is the time to dig in and "don't let the hill beat you".

Be on the lookout for those people who you might not know that can be your supporters, like the unexpected supporters on my run. People who will inspire you and help you tap into your inner strength and forge on.

Sometimes, even if you put your all into it, you might not get the desired result the first go round. It would be easy to think that you might never get to your finish line - you failed.

But what if these are just temporary setbacks and all your hard work and effort is not wasted, but instead it's just time to get still and refuel so you can go the next round?

These supposed failures might be the biggest learning opportunities you experience. If you feel like giving up on the dream or have in the past, here are a few examples of others who didn't let go of the dream and who "dug in" when the going got tough.

Milton Hershey failed in his first two attempts to set up a confectionary business and he went bankrupt.

Steve Jobs got fired from Apple, the company he founded.

Oprah Winfrey was once fired from her job as a reporter because she was "unfit for television".

Dr. Seuss's first book was rejected by publishers 27 times.

Bethany Hamilton, a surfer, was attacked by a shark and lost her arm and still went on to win first place in the Explorer Women's Division of the NSSA National Championships.

You probably have examples of everyday people in your own life who are dreaming big and digging in, who you can add to the list. Or what about the times in your life when you accomplished something that seemed almost impossible?

How did you "dig in" at those times? You can apply some of what you learned then to your current actions.

Dig in is about perseverance. I used to think that perseverance was all about withstanding suffering. In this situation though, perseverance is a form of validation of your purpose. It's not about suffering, it's about the opportunity to create, grow and make an impact. It's the ability to stay the course long enough, so all your efforts, talents and contributions to yourself and others, result in your big dreams coming to life.

Are you ready to take your life to the next level? Get prepared for the extraordinary and remarkable to occur, because that is what is going to happen when you dream big and dig in!

9

There, Now You Can't F--- it Up

A studio classroom with easels, tables, paints and the most amazing paintings on the wall – huge paintings. I stopped in front of one that I knew was from the Sistine Chapel. It was so mesmerizing that I could not believe what I was seeing.

"This is from one of our classes."

What? Could this be true?

"You teach people to paint like this? Like this?"

"Yes, we do."

"What kind of students come here?"

"Just average people who want to learn painting and some of our great techniques."

"Are they all professionals?"

"No, these classes are for everyone from novice to expert. We just teach differently than a traditional art class."

My mind was exploding and my whole body felt like it was buzzing with excitement. My brain was on fire!

"You teach people to paint like this? Here?"

Sign me up!

In that instant I knew that this was something I wanted more than anything and so I took the money and spent it on me – not for the house or the kids or my husband. It was just for me - because this was a life-long dream of mine.

I could not sleep the night before the class. I was so excited. That morning the energy in the studio was contagious. Sean Crosby, our instructor, was from New York, accent and all. We all went around the room and introduced ourselves.

To give you an idea of how excited I was, even though I was talking to everyone and heard their introductions, I didn't fully process that I was the only non-professional artist in the room.

Interestingly enough, Sean did not begin the class with an explanation of the technique. Instead, he started with a story of how he became an artist. Then he did something very surprising. He stopped and said,

"I don't usually do this but I feel that there's someone in this room that I'm supposed to help."

He shared some of his personal experiences with overcoming adversity in his life and he thought that perhaps he was there to inspire someone who was wrestling with a struggle of their own.

"So, I'm here for ya, if I can help." Then he simply switched gears and said, *"Okay, let's get goin."*

After Sean went over some techniques and his process, we went to our work stations to begin. I mixed up my paints, laid out all my brushes, and began to look at what the other participants were doing.

They were going to town. OMG – they weren't asking for help – just working so fast and confidently.

Then it started. That nagging thought that I couldn't get out of my head. I felt hot, scared, lost and I could feel tears welling up in my eyes.

Stupid, stupid, stupid girl. Who are you to think you can do this – you are such a dreamer. You're not qualified. These people are professionals and you're a nobody. You don't belong here. Stupid, stupid, stupid dreamer.

On the verge of a full blown panic attack, I was just about to flee from the room when suddenly Sean came up behind me.

"That's quite a nice work station ya got there".

"Oh thanks", I said nervously giggling to cover that I was scared shitless.

"I just want to make sure that I have everything laid out before I begin".

With one eyebrow raised and in the most skeptical tone, Sean said,

"Oh really? Ya been workin on it for about 20 minutes now."

Then he picked up one of the large brushes, dipped it in brown stain and swooshed it across my canvas.

"There – now ya can't fuck it up."

I just stood there with my mouth gaping open – stunned. He started to walk away while I stared after him, looking over his shoulder in the most nonchalant way.

"Ya might wanna wipe that off before it stains."

Yikes! I sprang into action and I dipped my rag in mineral spirits and put the rag to the canvas to wipe off the stain. Eureka – I was touching my canvas, taking action - what a genius and by far the best teacher I ever had.

I had wanted to be an artist since I was a child and dreamed of painting a masterpiece my whole life. But I took another path because of the story that I inherited from my mother. She did not think I could make a living as an artist because it was too risky for her tastes and naturally, she wanted to keep her child safe.

I took that belief on as my own, even though deep down inside I didn't really believe it. I mean, who doesn't want to be safe? But, I loved painting and drawing and in my spare time would paint on cardboard, paper anything I could get my hands on. For me it really wasn't a hobby, but that is where I delegated it because I doubted my calling.

So Sean was right, besides teaching us to paint a masterpiece, he was there to inspire and help someone overcome an internal struggle.

That day, in such a short interaction, I was liberated from my fear. The nagging voice that wanted to keep me small no longer had the same power over me and I had stepped into my light.

10

Accept Your Greatness

Our deepest fear is not that we are inadequate.
Our deepest fear is that we are powerful
beyond measure. It is our light, not our
darkness that most frightens us.
We ask ourselves, who am I to be brilliant,
gorgeous, talented, fabulous?

Marianne Williamson

Critical Connection #5

Accept Your Greatness

1. Your Greatness
2. Fear
3. Accepting Your Greatness

What if you were cleaning out a closet and found a rare, priceless masterpiece inside? How would that change your life?

What if you realized that there is a rare, priceless masterpiece inside of you? A one of a kind masterpiece, created by the most famous artist of all.

Your Greatness

Actually, God created you to be unique with tremendous greatness within, equipped with everything you need.

Everything about you matters and has value and there isn't another human being like you in the world. You are unique in your passions, talents, abilities and way of thinking and you're definitely not average or ordinary.

Think back to when you were a child and you embraced your greatness and had no trouble letting your light shine.

You trusted your natural curiosity to explore and experience the awe and wonder of the world around you. You wanted to build bridges, explore the North Pole, to be an artist, dancer, engineer, fireman, astronaut, president...nothing was off limits.

So what happened?

When did you succumb to the judgment of others or the limiting belief that you were not deserving, that you were ordinary? Perhaps your path of greatness was too hard and you began to have doubt or fear.

It happens to everyone at some point in their lives. You become conditioned to hide your greatness, to dim your light.

You think that you have to be a certain way before you can show your greatness, disqualifying yourself before you even get started. It sounds like this:

"I'm too fat to ..."

"I don't have a degree or credentials."

"I made too many past mistakes – bankruptcy, addiction, failed relationships, legal infractions..."

Fear

I did it too. At the moment when I signed up for the painting class, I was ready – could feel my greatness, my dream coming true.

But something happened during the morning of the class and quite frankly – my greatness scared the shit out of me!

I judged myself as lacking and not good enough – *who was I to think that I was worthy or talented?* With these thoughts I discounted my greatness and almost quit.

But no matter what you do, the greatness is still within you even if it is deeply layered over by limitations, rejections, fears, past failures and doubts.

All those layers just mean that you are human and vulnerable at times. Vulnerability is a sign of greatness because when you have the courage to face your fears and forgive your past, it no longer rules you. It takes confidence and let's others see just how strong you really are.

The only thing keeping you from accepting your greatness is you! You might have to do a little exploring *(Who do you want to be?)* so that you don't settle for mediocrity, but you can catapult yourself to where you want to be.

Accepting Your Greatness

You're probably amazingly quick in recognizing other people's greatness but not so much when it comes to your own. Even when other people point out something about you that is truly great, you down play it or brush it off. You can't accept it and without even realizing you pushed the dimmer switch.

It's okay to openly acknowledge our greatness, our contribution. Imagine if we all gave ourselves permission to say, "I was awesome today!" Dimming it down doesn't really make anyone else feel better.

People are drawn to confidence and love so when you step into your greatness, fully accepting yourself, you attract more people than you repel.

When you make the connection and "Accept Your Greatness" it's like a wakeup call reminding you of the treasure inside you –the God given potential you need to make your big dreams come true.

Just as no one else has your unique handprint, no one will ever leave a mark like yours.

So take this opportunity now to stop dimming the light of your greatness. Accept and embrace your greatness and let it radiate out to light the way as you step into your unlimited power.

The power to forge your own path and make your unique imprint on the world.

11

The Cake's No Good Without the Frosting, Helen

When I was a little girl my dad had a phrase that he would say to my mother quite a lot:

"The cake's no good without the frosting Helen."

Now, I just couldn't quite figure out why he was saying that to her. First of all I loved cake, but not with a lot of frosting. The other kids in my family, would fight over who was getting a corner piece of cake because they loved frosting, while I usually scraped mine off. So right off the bat I was at odds with the statement.

Secondly, when he said it my mother wasn't even making cake. Which was a disappointment in itself because my mother made the best cakes. Dessert was almost sacred in our house and the minute we heard cake, all of us kids went running to the kitchen in anticipation.

I can still remember feeling so disappointed, and from my viewpoint it wasn't very nice at all, the cruelest of jokes, to mention cake if there wasn't going to be any.

The other puzzling thing was that it was obvious from my mother's expression that she did not appreciate Daddy's opinion very much, but she would however stop her litany and switch to more pleasant topics.

Even though at the time I couldn't really understand what it meant, I was intuitive enough to pick up that it must be something important because he said it a lot.

I can hear his voice clearly when I think of it, although I cannot really see his face anymore just an impression of his body language.

As an adult, it has had a profound impact on me as I realized what he had done and the importance of that saying in the moment.

By nature my mother is dramatic with a tendency to be on the nervous side and no doubt, parenting 10 children contributed greatly to her stress.

She took her job as a mother very seriously and I have to say that sometimes we were an adventurous bunch of kids – ok, most of the time.

Her level of worry could sky rocket from something small to a future catastrophe in a matter of minutes.

I'm not sure how it happened, but she had fallen into the unconscious habit of verbalizating her worries of what could go wrong, her numerous regrets of the past and her limitations.

Daddy worked two jobs which left my mother holding down the homefront most of the time. It was probably how my mother fell into that mode. She only had a few minutes to tell him what she was worried about. So she capitalized on the moment to express her fears. But she was so entrenched in the habit that she was doing it whether Daddy was there or not.

I'm pretty sure that my dad didn't want his few minutes with the family to be focused on the negative either. He wanted to enjoy being with us in the moment and to spend some happy time with my mother, who he loved dearly.

Instead of making her feel bad, Daddy came up with a friendly cue – to shift her from worry wart mode. A cue that would mean something to her, which could stop her from focusing on the negative to focusing on what was good in the current moment.

My mother has a sweet tooth that I am sure could be recorded in the Guiness Book of World Records. I have never met anyone who craves sugary desserts as much and unbelievably not become ill. It's probably why she became such an awesome baker. So as you can see, frosting was something she understood and related to on a deep level.

This was my dad's way to help my mother reframe from the negative to the positive without undermining her in front of her children. To help her recognize and celebrate the "sweet spots" that were right before her.

Now that I am a coach, I clearly recognize his innate ability to reframe so naturally. I also recognize my mother's ability to willingly shift once she was cued in to her "negative speak" which shows her tremendous strength as well.

It had become a blind spot for her, so having someone who loved and respected her and, who presented the message the way she could hear it, allowed her to pause and choose how she wanted to go forward.

As an adult I found myself following in my mother's footsteps during times of high stress. Let's face it, kids hear what their parents say and do, and that becomes the model of life for them until or unless there are other life experiences to help them shift out of the default mode.

Unfortunately for our family, my father passed away when I was 9 years old so he wasn't there to shift me out of default stress mode. But one day, I received a message that reminded me that I can reframe myself and find the frosting on my cake of life, in the current moment.

I walked into the kitchen and my husband had done the dishes, but he left crumbs and spills on the counters and the sinks were filthy. I just couldn't understand why he never finished the job. I didn't realize that anyone was around and I was saying out loud in my frustration:

"I can't believe this, again – how many times have I told him that he never finishes and I can't stand cleaning out the sinks after the crud has been sitting there. C'mon how hard can it be to wipe off a counter?"

When all of a sudden from the other side of the room, came a high, falsetto voice mocking me,

"You're such a jerk Steve. You did all the dishes which is the hardest part and now all I have to do is wipe off the counters. How inconsiderate!"

No, it wasn't my husband, it was my 14 year old son who I had not seen lying on the couch. His delivery was so spot on that I started to laugh instantly, but the message was received loud and clear. What a great way to reframe the situation and I could just imagine my father saying,

"The cake's no good without the frosting, Suzy."

When I came into the kitchen, I had focused on what I perceived to be the negative, the sour spots, instead of the nice thing that my husband had done.

I had literally scraped off the frosting from my husband's cake and in so doing from my son's as well.

So now when I find myself getting a little stressed out, I have a giant metaphorical piece of cake and I load it up with plenty of frosting.

A few years later I received an unexpected validation that I was truly living with the sweet spots of life in mind and leaving an imprint that I was proud of, when my husband sent me flowers with a card that read:

"You are the frosting on the cake of my life."

12

Focus on the Current Opportunity

It's being here now that's important. There's no past and there's no future. Time is a very misleading thing. All there is ever, is the now.

George Harrison

Critical Connection #6

Focus on the Current Opportunity

1. The Sweet Spot
2. Disconnecting
3. Connecting
4. The Current Opportunity

To focus on the current opportunity means to live in the present when life is developing right before your eyes. Even though life can be considered in timeframes, a progression of moments, marking time is not the same as making "it" your mark. It is the exact opposite.

The Sweet Spot

If your focus is predominately on what has passed or what is to come, you could find yourself missing "it" – the sweet spot – the point where you have the most influence and impact.

The time to create your imprint and make "it" your mark is happening right now. Each moment gives you the opportunity and time to enjoy what you are doing, to delight in the people around you - to leave your imprint.

What is cool about this is that when you raise your awareness and focus on what is happening in the moment, you have the power and opportunity to choose your response or action. This is the point where you have the most ability to maximize your impact.

What happened a moment ago is in the past and the future hasn't happened. It's what you do right now that makes the difference.

In my mother's case in the previous story, she was so focused on the past and the future that she was robbing herself of the joy that was all around her. The proverbial frosting in her life.

But when she shifted out of her default stress mode, she became aware of what she was doing and in that instant, could make a change. To show up in a way that was aligned to who she really wanted to be.

Trust me, she was not a person who considered herself to be a victim, but I am sure there were times that she felt at the mercy of what was occurring in her life.

Whining and complaining was not something that she tolerated in her kids, and so when my dad helped her recognize that she was in essence in complaint mode, she quickly chose to reframe her words.

That is what focusing on the current opportunity is all about. Becoming aware of what is going on in the moment, so you can experience it, choose how to respond and act so that you show up the way you want to be.

Disconnecting

It's easy to slip into a state of disconnection with the present, if you're preoccupied with worrying about the future and ruminating about your past regrets.

Think about a time when you were under stress, maybe you couldn't sleep for several nights because a worrying thought was running through your head.

When you're under stress, especially prolonged stress, you can slip into a default mode of behavior. It's like having a huge blind spot blocking out your ability to see options or connections.

This can result in a type of tunnel vision, limiting your decision making opportunities, your ability to be in the moment because you are oblivious to anything outside of the tunnel.

But this kind of mindless disconnection can be insidious, easily pouring over into your normal day to day way of being if you're not aware. Here are a few examples illustrating how this can happen:

1. *Have you ever been talking to someone, sharing something deep and important, to have them stop and say, "I'm sorry, what was that?" Or worse, their cell phone rings or buzzes and they actually pick it up and either take the call or start texting while you're talking. Oblivious to the fact they just created a disconnection.*

   Of course, they tell you they're sorry and to go on, but did you really feel like they cared? How'd it make you feel? If you're like most people, you might be willing to let it go a time or two, but after that it leaves a negative mark with you.

   Maybe you've done this yourself when someone was talking to you.

2. *The boss comes in and just walks past your desk or office without a greeting, wave, or any indication that they realize you are there.*

   You call out, "Hello" or "Good Morning" and maybe get a nod or a grunt, but no real response. You might have thought they were just busy or preoccupied.

   But what if it happened every day, the same kind of dismissive interaction. You probably start to feel a little taken for granted. What if they never took the initiative to speak first and greet you? What kind of mark is being created in that moment?

3. *What about being so preoccupied, that when your child wants to show you a painting they did, you barely glance at it and say something like, "That's nice. I'm real busy right now - go play with your toys."*

You're so mindlessly disconnected that you don't even see the hurt look in your child's eyes and the sadness on their face. Then later on, you actually look at the picture and it is of you with a beautiful message about how much you are loved.

You inadvertently lost a moment to feel and be loved by someone very special and you might have taught them that they're not important to you as well.

These moment by moment interactions you have with people in your life tell them more about you than you might think. The reality you are creating by your actions might not be the one you want.

Connecting

Imagine if you embraced every moment and you gave your full attention to everything you did and every person you came in contact with in that moment.

How would that align with your vision, values, and voice? What kind of difference would result in the reality you want to create?

How different would it be if instead, in that few minutes of someone sharing their thoughts with you, you made the commitment to fully connect? All the distractions were put to the side and you gave them your full attention and focus.

One of the comments that my clients make all the time is how wonderful it was to have someone really listen to them and not interrupt them. To let them share what they think and feel without judgment for a few minutes.

What if you looked at the picture and took a few minutes to hug your child and let them know you loved them, leaving an imprint in their heart that they were important and significant?

Stopping in the moment and taking the opportunity to connect, maximizes your impact and helps you ensure that you are leaving an imprint that represents your purpose.

Focus on the Current Opportunity

Relishing each moment in life allows you to expand its value and make it more meaningful. You find the frosting and all the other sweet spots.

When you push your focus into the present, you can't think about the past or worry about what isn't there yet in the future. Mindless disconnection can kill your momentum and keep you from taking necessary action to achieve your dreams.

One of the quickest ways to free yourself from mindless disconnection is to let go of the past and to trust in the future. The past is done and no matter how much you might want to go back and change it, you can't.

When you hold on to those painful memories, mistakes, struggles and problems, perceived hurts and wrong doings, you actually bring them into the present.

You rob yourself of the chance to do things differently now. To take what you learned from all of your life experiences and apply that learning in a more positive, purposeful way.

Even though you can't go back, you can move on and regain your momentum. How in the world could you know everything you "should" know without making mistakes and experiencing some stumbles in your life?

In hindsight, it's easy to see the things that could have been done differently. But in the moment you make the best decision you can with the information you have then. Forgive yourself for not being all knowing and powerful. You're human after all and making mistakes is all part of living and learning.

Your past is one part of who you are, but it is not the sum of who you are and not all of your past has negative connotations. Think of the wisdom you are acquiring as you go through the hard lessons in life.

I can't help but think of the song from the Disney movie, Frozen – "Let it go, let it go"! Don't let your past hold you back from living a full and satisfying life.

Which is why focusing on the current moment is so great. Perhaps your past has a very strong hold on you, think of this as a way to "baby" step into a new way of being. You don't have to transform your thinking all at once, just one moment at a time.

Future directed thinking is related to outcomes, and it is important to think and vision for what you want to happen, to build a framework to support your goals.

However, if you are worried about the future or become so focused on the outcome, you could be closing yourself off from the opportunity you have right now to positively impact your future.

By its very nature, worry is future related and when you consciously raise your awareness to the current moment, worry dissolves.

When you concentrate your attention on the present, you focus on the task at hand. You give your full attention to what you're doing and you let go of the outcome.

You begin with a vision of the future, "begin" being the operative word here. You want to have a specific idea of where you want to go and then shift your focus to the process of getting there. Otherwise, it is just dreaming.

Trust in the future and let go of the outcome so you can focus in the place where you have the most control and influence – the current moment – the present.

Focusing on the current opportunity is action oriented whether taking a moment to be still to collect yourself or engaging in the task at hand. When you are purposeful and focused it fuels your momentum in achieving your goals and creating the "SWEET" life you desire.

13

Chalkboard Messages from Tinton Falls

When I lived in New Jersey, I drove to work through a little town called Tinton Falls. The street that I drove on each day was quaint with old farmhouses and colonials adding to the small town charm.

There was one house in particular that stood out, not so much for its architecture or landscaping, but for the large chalkboard sign erected next to the curb.

Each morning I couldn't help seeing the messages hand written in chalk for all the commuters to read. Some could be short like "Choose harmony" or "You are worthy" or thought provoking with "Let go of old beliefs" or "Fear Not"...

These messages were motivational and positive, and so often had a direct connection to what was going on in my life, that I almost stopped one day to ask the people how they knew what was happening to me.

It was better than Facebook and on the days when there wasn't a message posted, I was almost a little sad.

One of the reasons that the messages were so meaningful was that I had just moved to New Jersey for a career opportunity with no guarantee that it would work out like I wanted. Also, my family was in Texas and my husband left his career to go with me.

Not afraid of taking risks, we just decided to gamble on the opportunity and have an adventure by living in a different part of the country. I had never lived in a place that actually had four seasons, and was excited to experience all the new things.

When we started to settle in, it was clear that I was far more pleased with the move than my husband. He had to find a new job and I already had one, so we experienced very different comfort levels.

He was homesick and so hard hit, I had never seen him like this in our 20+ years together. Maybe we were just too set in our ways for this much adventure. I had always thought my purpose was to inspire, but I was doubting that this move was very inspirational considering how uncomfortable it felt.

One morning as I was driving to work, I was thinking about our situation and wondering if I had made the right decision of uprooting us and moving across the country. Was I really connected to a purposeful path? I was praying for some kind of sign of what to do when I noticed the big chalkboard.

In large print, written at a slant was this message:

"Inspiration comes when you get out of your comfort zone."

Hmmm. Seemed like the sign was meant for me, because if two people were ever out of their comfort zones that would have to be us. I began to feel much better about the decision to move to Jersey and soon we both began to appreciate the feeling of community, the sites and activities of our new state.

Each week the messages spoke to me at the times when I needed it most, and I became very curious about the mysterious scribe who lived in the old farmhouse.

Clearly there was a purpose to the messages and the act of writing them for all to see. So I started asking around to see if anyone knew the owners of the house.

I found an article in the paper about the owner, a man who holds a doctorate in divinity and philosophy, who had been posting messages for years. Three times a week he changed the message on the board, to help commuters feel better about themselves, relax a little and take time to appreciate life.

There are too many to list, but as I reflected on what the messages meant to me it made me think about other times in my life when I received messages that were powerful and relevant. Signs that helped me grow and learn – that validated my purpose and had great impact on my life and my relationships.

It was so powerful - this seemingly small act by one man who did not know if his messages would make an impression or not, but who had a calling to post them anyway. His purpose to simply help people feel better about themselves and to appreciate life.

It's a curious thing, trying to figure out your purpose and use your voice. I used to think it had to be BIG, huge like a Hollywood epic movie theme and that I would receive some kind of monumental sign pointing me in the right direction.

I hear that same thing from my clients, who are waiting for a sign to validate what they think their purpose really is. They think they had a sign, but are just not sure.

Could a sign be that small and soft – shouldn't it be thunderous, of Biblical proportions? Maybe we just resist the sign and that's why it doesn't seem thunderous or momentous.

We're conditioned to be doubtful and with all the hustle and bustle in our lives, how good is our hearing anyway? But the signs of people who are stating their purpose very simply in their actions and their words are all around us.

Mother Teresa is a good example of this, because she basically wanted to help the poor, started one person at a time and ended up having tremendous global influence and impact over the course of her life. She wasn't waiting, she was taking purposeful action – making a huge impact.

So is the Chalkboard Messenger in Tinton Falls. He purposefully shares a simple, inspirational message 3 or 4 times a week to all those who drive down his street. Over the past 14 years, he has touched thousands of lives with his inspiration, playing a part in our daily lives and making a lasting impression.

Perhaps you are one of the many who are wondering if you have found your purpose, but are waiting for a bigger sign. You are thinking that your purpose seems too simple and feel silly if you share it with others.

But whenever you stop and ask yourself, " What is my purpose in life?" and you keep getting the same answer; I share this message from Tinton Falls with you in the hope that it calls you to action like it has for so many others:

14

Use Your Voice

In life, finding a voice is speaking and living the truth. Each of you is an original. Each of you has a distinctive voice. When you find it, your story will be told. You will be heard.

John Grisham

Critical Connection #7

Use Your Voice

1. An Uplifting Plot
2. Speak Up!

Your voice is the third component for keeping yourself in the purpose zone. Your voice has tremendous influence in your life as you use it to reveal your purpose, to describe your vision, make an impact and to align your values.

It's like your very own chalkboard, broadcasting your purpose to the world and leaving your imprint on the people and places in your life.

An Uplifting Plot

The messages you create and the words you share create your authentic story – your truest self. For that reason, one of the most important elements of your voice is choosing the words and messages that align with who you want to be and how you want to show up.

Inner messages and words, inner speak, have the most influence. These inner messages can be simple, yet carry tremendous weight like the chalkboard messages from the previous chapter.

As you consider your inner speak, ask yourself these questions:

How uplifting are your inner messages?

How well do they reveal who you want to be and how you want to show up?

If you think you might need to do a little "rewriting", then this is a great time for you jump into the author seat and do some edits, so you- the main character, resonate authentically.

One way to create an inner speak that builds you up and motivates you is to practice a simple affirmation daily. Your personal "chalkboard message".

The word affirmation originates from the Latin word, affirmare, which means "to make steady, strengthen."

A self-affirmation sets the tone for the day and helps you honor and engage your great gifts and talents. As you create your affirmations and use them, your thoughts and intentions will begin to manifest into your desired actions. Actions that can have tremendous impact on the people you encounter in the day to day.

When you develop your self-affirmations, use your answers to the questions, *"Who do you want to be?"* and *"How do you want to show up?"*

Here's some examples of self-affirmations that you can use:

I am an inspiration to the people in my life.

I am confident, open-minded, and engaging.

I am a powerful person who makes a difference in the lives of others.

I am a change agent, pushing the boundaries of my comfort zone.

I am worthy and valuable.

I am a beautiful person inside and out.

I am innovative and find solutions to my challenges.

I am the architect of my life.

I am bursting with energy and joy.

I have everything I need I to make my big dreams come true.

I am meant to use my greatness to make a contribution to the world.

I am important, worthy, and valuable and deserve abundance and prosperity.

I am blessed with an incredible family and wonderful friends.

You get the idea. You can use any of these, create new ones, or tweak these to fit your personal needs. Some people have a new affirmation for each day, others have one for each week and still others have one a month. It's just a matter of personal preference, the important thing is to use them.

You'll discover that when you make your daily affirmation, people will begin commenting on how great you look today or what an awesome idea you had, etc. That's because, when you use your voice you show up the way you want to be.

Speak Up!

You have an important message and contribution to share with the world, so take the opportunity and speak up! This is the second way you use your voice to influence your life and maximize your impact—how you make "it" your mark.

All through history, stories have been used to teach and inform. The human interest story is one of the most intriguing, because people love to hear about other people. We connect to stories of people who overcame tragedy, who showed courage, or who made their dreams come true, because seeing someone else triumph triggers an emotional response that there is hope for us all.

Your stories, the ones about your experiences or the ones you've collected along the way, can also provide a means of connection. You never know who might need your unique perspective. The ideas you have might give them hope or help them as they create their mark.

When you speak up authentically, the way you want to be and how you want to show up, you will leave the imprint you want in the people and things in your life.

That is what happened in Tinton Falls with the chalkboard messenger from the previous chapter. He used his voice – his influence – on a daily basis and his mark lit up the road for all who drove down it to see.

Yours can too.

In Closing

My hope is you will take what you have learned here and use it daily to help you maximize your impact and create the lasting impression you want to make on the world.

Before you go, there is one more item that needs your attention and focus and that is your life purpose statement.

Your life purpose statement is a brief declaration, usually only a sentence or two, that comes from your core being. It states your mission or calling, the contribution that you feel you are meant to give the world. It is the key to maximizing your impact.

You'll want to think about this for a little while and try out a few before you land on the one that feels right for you. As you do, keep in mind that your purpose can be stated quite simply and still have a deep and meaningful impact.

Review your vision, values and affirmations to see what words or pictures jump off the page at you. In this exercise, remember to accept your greatness, because it is quite common for humility to kick in. But you want to embrace your greatness so that your purpose is authentic, powerful and strong as it becomes the guide in your life.

You were meant to be great and to share your purpose with others, so jump in and boldly create yours. There is no right way to phrase your purpose, so use your voice because this needs to have your authentic handprint all over it!

Not sure how to get it started? You can begin with a simple opening such as:

"My purpose is to ..."

Then you can add to it if you choose. These are some examples to help you get your creative process going:

My purpose is to be kind and loving.

I am a healing presence in the world.

My purpose is to serve – myself and others.

My purpose is to laugh often, learn always, and to love.

Here's mine: I inspire.

That's it, and yet it can touch so many areas and people. What do I inspire in others? I am not always aware, but that is what I love about it, there are no limits on who, how, when, or where I inspire!

Once you've created your purpose statement, you'll want to see it in your actions. Then when you look back on your life and wonder,

What is my legacy? What bit of evidence did I leave behind that says, "I was here."?

You will know the contribution you purposefully choose to give, to maximize your impact.

Are you ready to go and Make it YOUR Mark? To be the person you want to be and leave a lasting impression on your world?

Well get ready and hold on because it is going to be an amazing ride.

You begin with two simple questions:

Who do I want to be?

And how do I want to show up?

John Bond

John Bond

Jerry Trevino Sr.

Jerry Trevino Jr. with his father.

Jerry Trevino Jr. with his son.

My brother David.

My brother David playing at Easter.

Me, crossing the finish line!

A sweet spot for my mother and father.

My painting.

Sean Crosby and I.

Attend a Live Make it YOUR Mark training session!

Take what you learned in the book to an even more powerful level by attending a Make it YOUR Mark live training and meet Susan in person.

In just two days, you will learn skills and tools that you can use right away to put your purpose into action!

Reserve your seat at
www.MakeItYourMark.com

Here's what participants are saying about the live Make it YOUR Mark training:

"It reinforced what is important in my life and I gained insight on a belief that was holding me back. Make it YOUR Mark has helped me visualize my priorities."

Carmen Bernal – HR Recruiter, UPS

"I learned things I didn't know I needed, but am so glad that I have them now to live according to what I value. Great training and it was good to meet new people."

Jim Earl – Independent Contractor

"This weekend, I broke through so many limiting beliefs I have been carrying. Now I know that I choose, not others. I recommend this training to everyone!"

Katherine De La Vega - PhD

"I took away so much that I can use in my personal life and also with my work colleagues. Especially about being still and listening on a deep level. I was connected to what was in my heart. This was so much more than I expected."

Brian Mittelstadt – Technology Project Manager, Simplify, Inc.

"This training gave me a guide to help me set priorities/goals that I want to achieve as there will always be new things to accomplish - keep moving forward and upward!"

Patty Escobedo – Executive Director Southwest ISD

"One small change in thinking can change your life. I learned so much and now feel like I have the steps to fulfilling my purpose. You are an awesome coach Susan and this weekend was just what I needed."

Suzuka Ballentine, Owner – Life with Photos

"I gained a lot of confidence this weekend and was surprised at how powerful and emotional it was to recognize your deepest gifts and talents. The interaction with the other participants was fun and the weekend went by so fast. Loved it!"

Kathleen Hilsher – Realtor

"I was surprised and deeply moved at how powerful it was to see my vision written. I also uncovered some thought patterns that I need to release to be more open and accepting."

Helen Wilson – Chief Financial Officer

"Working in a people focused job, this training helped me reconnect with strengths and talents that I have and enhanced those skills. I realized that we could all use this type of training to increase our awareness of the bad or default habits we take on so we can make sure that we stay connected with the most positive behaviors."

Henry Bernal – Social Worker, Harlandale ISD

"On day two of the training it really began to sink in that I can change anything that I want to! I believed this before, but the activities in the training took it to another level of empowerment for me."

Barbara Evers - Homemaker

"I gained the confidence and skills to move toward a better and brighter future. "

Christina Kaiser – Office Manager

"The training is set up in such a way that I no longer wanted to escape from the tough issues I have been struggling with. I can control my choices and what I learned can be applied to all areas of my life.

Tamra Urbach – General Manager, Allegra SA

26991177R00071

Made in the USA
Middletown, DE
09 December 2015